Mount Everest
8,849m 29,032 ft

For my daughter, Emi —A.Y.

For my mother, who graduated from Showa Women's University just like Junko,
when few Japanese women pursued higher education —Y.S.

UP, UP, EVER UP!

JUNKO TABEI : A Life in the Mountains

Words by **ANITA YASUDA**

Art by **YUKO SHIMIZU**

CLARION BOOKS
An Imprint of HarperCollinsPublishers

Junko's hill was her entire world.

Under its sakura trees, she'd lie on the cool grass, listening. Stories of mountains drifted all around her until silvery domes and icy peaks unfurled as far as she could see. As the mountains took shape, a dream formed within Junko: to climb.

When she turned ten, Junko and her friends climbed Mount Chausu step-by-step. Hot springs sizzled, ears pricked, and Junko's nose scrunched at the egg-scented air. A slope bristling with boulders urged:

Up, up, and ever up!

Junko wondered where else she might explore. But a life of climbing mountains seemed as far away as the sky they braced.

When Junko left her home in Miharu for the grayscape of concrete, she shuffled with the *gatan-goton* of rumbling Tokyo trains. But her heart longed for the mountains, whitecaps on a deep, deep sea.

Even though most mountaineering clubs said "No Women Allowed," Junko found one that said "Yes!"

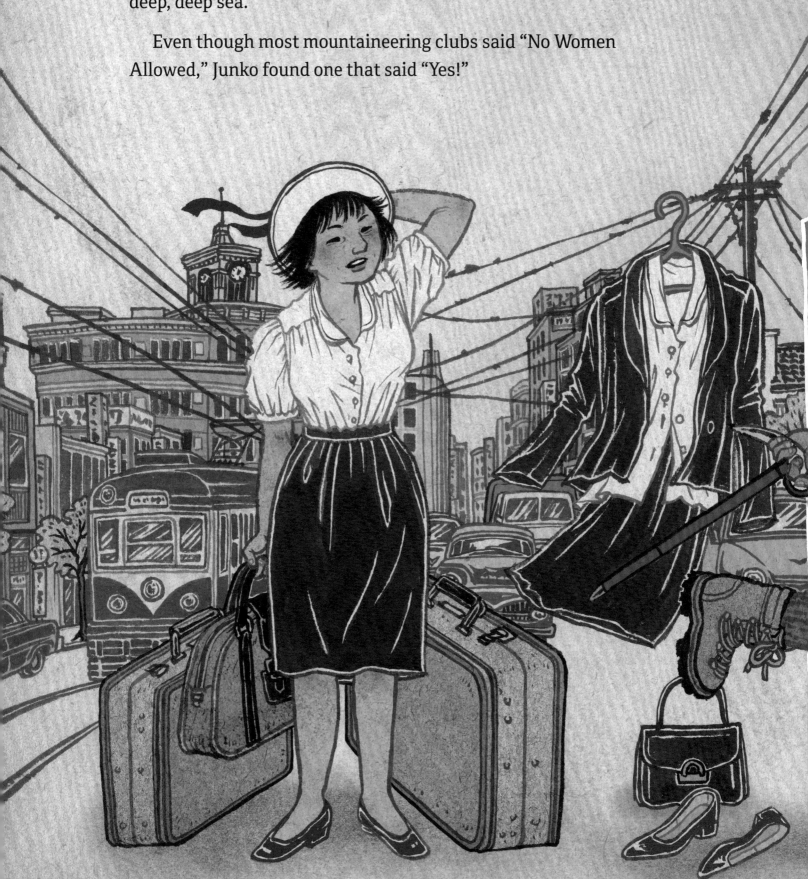

Each weekend, she laced her boots for where streams ran smooth and silent and mists revealed rocky spurs and granite knolls.

With harness and rope, she reached and slipped and reached again until the landscape was part of her. Finding joy on

camel ridges,

cloud catchers,

and craters wide and flat.

She met someone who loved mountains as much as she did. They married and became a family of three peaks.

As her family grew, Junko knitted other women climbers together, just as a ridge joins mountaintops. Like her, they wanted opportunities above the clouds. Eager and unstoppable, they planned, trained, and dreamed beyond the horizon.

They plotted an expedition to the world's highest mountain, Everest. A challenge so great only a few people had ever succeeded, and *no* women had. "Ganbarimasu!" The women believed they could do it.

Step-by-step.

When sponsors told Junko "Stay home and raise your child," she became a mother who climbed *for* her daughter.

Up, up, and ever up!

Junko and the team recycled what they had . . .

. . . into what they needed.

When mountaineering gloves
didn't fit because they were made
only for men, Junko sewed her
own and fashioned pants from
her okaasan's kimono lining.

After years of preparation, Junko and her fellow climbers landed in Nepal. Their excitement met with a tumble of open markets and air thick as a mug of butter tea.

A group of Sherpas from the bustling city of Kathmandu and the high hills of Namche Bazaar joined the trailblazing expedition.

Day by day, word spread of the first all-women team . . .

. . . until Nepali people, some mothers like Junko, came from villages as far away as a three-day walk to carry the team's fifteen tons of gear. Soon the rhythm of over five hundred porters, aunties, uncles, younger brothers, and big sisters swayed over bridges and rumbled past painted chortens.

Among the jangle of yak bells and the grunt of voices, Junko trekked through dusty villages and blue pine forests.

The wind whispered prayers for a safe climb as Everest's summit rose before her.

Up, up, and ever up!

The team spent weeks establishing camps
beyond the maze of moving ice and deep
crevasses of the Khumbu Icefall until Everest
awoke, and . . .

Blocks of ice and rock
slammed into Junko
and her four tentmates,
tossing them
down,

down,

down.

Pinned within her tent, fighting
for air, Junko saw a vision of her
family, of her daughter. She had to
stay alive for them. She had to stay
alive for *herself*.

Sherpas escaped, and, despite the
danger, they clawed at the wall of
ice. A hand, a head, a boot! They dug
until they freed each climber.

Everywhere Junko looked lay gear, strewn like the stars above. Worse, she could barely stand.

Junko's gaze followed the team's koinobori flag: the wind dragging it down the mountain, the carp refusing to give up.

With enough oxygen for two people, only the group's climbing leader, Junko, and her guide, Ang Tsering Sherpa, would attempt Everest's summit. Could Junko accomplish what no woman had before?

Almost two weeks later, they reached their last camp. Waves of wind rattled their tent like a tiny vessel on a wild ocean. Before dawn, Junko began her ascent.

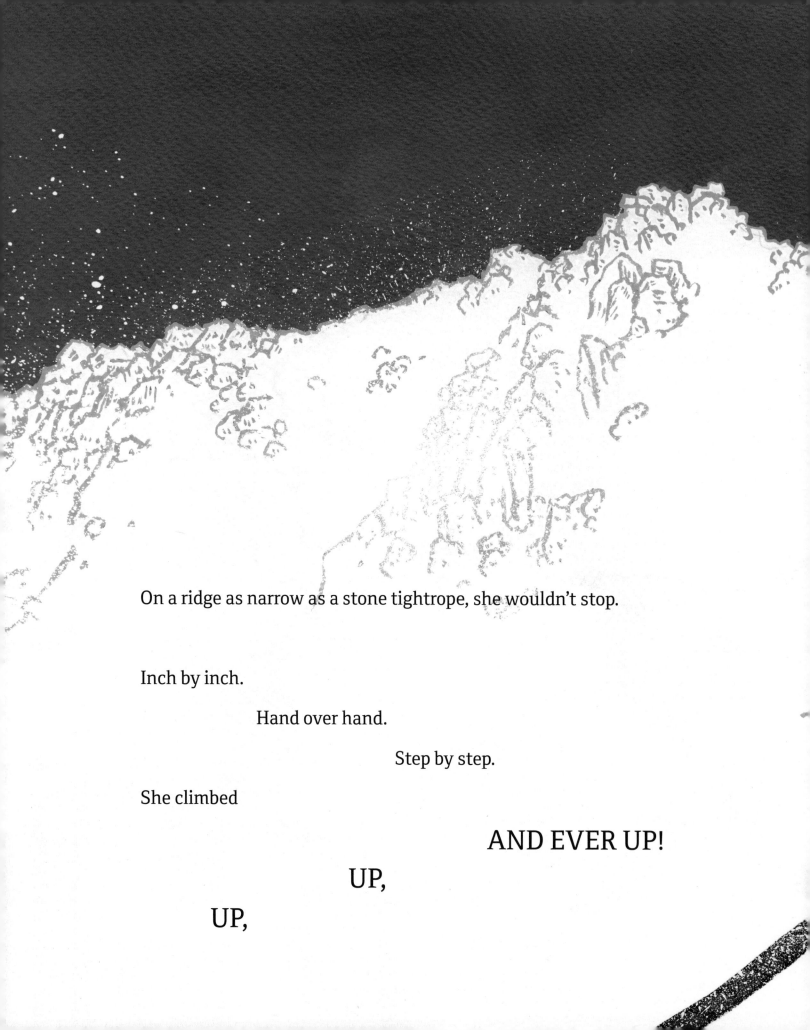

On a ridge as narrow as a stone tightrope, she wouldn't stop.

Inch by inch.

Hand over hand.

Step by step.

She climbed

AND EVER UP!

UP,

UP,

Junko stood on Everest's summit, where earth met sky:

silvery domes

and icy peaks

unfurled as far as she could see.

On a snowy patch, no larger than a tatami mat, she gazed upon a landscape untouched by people. Just two small climbers in a cloud of white.

Like a mighty glacier, Junko continued carving paths for women, one peak at a time, from China to Argentina. But she never stopped thinking about the beauty of the Himalayas.

As the years rose, crumpled, and folded into the next, thousands followed in her footsteps. In Nepal, trash climbed as high as the swirling clouds that wreathed Everest.

Discarded tents fluttered like feathery birch bark under the shimmering sun, and oxygen canisters blazed on the ice as if autumn had tinted the Himalayas.

A promise rose within Junko.
"Yaritai!" She would help.

Sherpas and sirdars.

Porters and people.

The Everest she loved.
Beneath pine tapestries,
she collected litter from the
Mani stone trail left by
climbers, porters, and
caravans of yaks.

In tiny villages hemmed by terraced fields and forests, Junko planted apple seedlings that reminded her of home. Maybe the lives of the people would improve as the lush orchards grew.

Then she urged the protection of mountain ecosystems. At environmental conferences, her words illuminated

cool grass and hot springs,

slopes and summits.

Because she was always that
young girl on her first mountain.

Reaching the top, step-by-step.
Up, up, and ever up!

AUTHOR'S NOTE

Junko Tabei once said, "I needed to climb and to be among the peaks. The rocky landscape had become a part of me." She was as devoted and passionate about mountain climbing as she was about preserving the natural landscapes she loved so much.

Concerned about the impact of climbing on the environment, Junko campaigned for sustainable mountaineering. In her late fifties, she returned to college. There, she researched the effect of garbage and human waste on Mount Everest. Junko interviewed solo climbers and members of large international expeditions. She returned to Base Camp twenty-five years after summiting Mount Everest. In Nepal, she weighed climbing waste, investigated the problem of night soil, and put her findings into her master's thesis for Kyushu University. She suggested that the number of Everest climbers be controlled and that climbers think about waste disposal before their ascent.

Inspired by the humanitarian work of Sir Edmund Hillary, who, along with Tenzing Norgay Sherpa, were the first mountaineers on Everest's summit, she devoted herself to keeping mountains free of pollution. In 1990, Junko became head of the Himalayan Adventure Trust of Japan (HAT-J), a nonprofit environmental group. Members encouraged public awareness about waste in Japan through organized "Take in–Take out" campaigns on popular hiking trails. They also organized teams of Nepali volunteers to clean up garbage left behind by climbers and expeditions on Everest. They built the first incinerator, a plant that burns garbage, in Lukla, Nepal—a task made more difficult by port strikes in India, where the equipment was shipped, and a lack of infrastructure in Nepal.

From the mid-1990s, HAT-J planted Fuji, Obayashi, Sunshine, and New Jonagold apple seedlings in the Eastern region of Nepal, including Chaurikharka and Cheplung, and initiated farming student exchanges between Japan and Nepal. Junko believed the fruit might become an important source of income for Nepali women, who could sell the apples to trekkers and bakeries around Namche Bazaar.

When Nepal needed someone to represent their mountains, wildlife, and culture abroad, they chose Junko to be their goodwill ambassador. She campaigned for responsible tourism. At environmental conferences, Junko explained that Everest "needed a rest now."

In 2011, after the Great East Japan earthquake, tsunami, and nuclear disaster in the prefecture of Fukushima, Junko worked with survivors. She rushed aid to them, including blankets and jackets. She opened her ski lodge to evacuees, saying that she knew how to survive challenges after Everest. Junko also organized an annual Mount Fuji hike for high school students in the affected region, teaching them the importance of conservation and rebuilding their love of nature.

In 2016, three months after hiking with students on the annual Mount Fuji hike, Junko passed away. It was her last climb. But Junko's commitment to mountain environments lives on through her work and a trust established by her son, Shinya. The Junko Tabei Foundation encourages all people to discover and care for the mountains. Junko's remarkable life inspires others to pursue their dreams, step-by-step, up, up, and ever up!

TIMELINE

1852 Surveyors determine that Peak XV (Mount Everest, also known as Chomolungma in Tibetan or Sagarmatha in Sanskrit) is the highest mountain on earth.

1939 Junko (Ishibashi) Tabei is born in Miharu, Fukushima Prefecture, Japan, on September 22.

1949 Discovers her love of climbing on a trip to the Nasu Mountain Range.

1958–62 Studies at Showa Women's University in Tokyo and continues climbing mountains.

1967 Marries fellow mountaineer, Masanobu Tabei; they later have two children, Noriko and Shinya.

1969 Establishes the Women's Climbing Club (Joshi-Tohan Club).

1970 Reaches the summit of Annapurna III in the Himalayas on the Women's Climbing Club's first expedition abroad.

1971 Forms the Japanese Women's Everest Expedition with fourteen other members of the Women's Climbing Club.

1972 Receives a permit for a 1975 Mount Everest trek.

1975 Summits Mount Everest on May 16, the first woman to achieve this feat. Nepal awards her with the Order of the Gorkha Dakshina Bahu, one of its highest honors.

1982 Publishes her autobiography, *Everest Mother*, the first of many books about her climbing adventures.

1990 Forms a branch of the Himalayan Adventure Trust in Japan.

1992 Conquers the seven summits (Everest, Aconcagua, Denali, Kilimanjaro, Elbrus, Vinson, and Puncak Jaya), a first for women.

1995 Receives a Japanese prime minister's award for achievements made toward gender equality.

2000 Graduates from the Graduate School of Social and Cultural Studies, Kyushu University, and speaks at the International Symposium on the Himalayan Environments.

2007 Receives a special award from the International Climbing and Mountaineering Federation (UIAA) for her contribution to international mountaineering.

2009 Establishes the MJ Link (Mountain Josei) organization that encourages young women to enjoy mountaineering.

2015 Works as a goodwill ambassador for Nepal after a severe earthquake strikes the country.

2016 Dies on October 20, having climbed the highest mountains in more than seventy countries.

2017 Junko Tabei's humanitarian work continues through the establishment of the Junko Tabei Foundation.

2019 The International Astronomical Union names a mountain range on Pluto "Tabei Montes," in honor of Junko Tabei.

GLOSSARY

avalanche when a mass of snow, earth, or ice breaks free from a mountainside

butter tea tea made with yak butter

chorten Buddhist shrine

koinobori carp-shaped wind sock

gatan-goton Japanese onomatopoeia for the sound of a train

Ganbarimasu "We will give it our best"

glacier slow-moving mass of ice, snow, and sediment

okaasan mother

sakura cherry blossoms

Sherpa a member of a Himalayan people known for their mountaineering skills

sirdar a Sherpa leader on a mountaineering expedition

summit highest part of a mountain

Yaritai "I want to do it"

SOURCE NOTES

I would like to thank Kazunori Tagami for his assistance and providing me with details on Himalayan Adventure Trust—Japan's environmental and humanitarian work in Nepal; Setsuko Kitamura, member of the Japan Women's Everest Expedition of 1975; translator Yumiko Hiraki, who kindly shared her memories of Junko Tabei; Dr. Teiji Watanabe, Hokkaido University; the Japanese Alpine Club; Journal of the Physical Society of Japan; and Kul Bahadur Gurung, general secretary of the Nepal Mountaineering Association (NMA).

SELECT BIBLIOGRAPHY

Bumiller, Elisabeth. "At the Peak of Her Profession." *Washington Post*, April 8, 1991. https://www.washingtonpost.com/archive/lifestyle/1991/04/08/at-the-peak-of-her-profession/ffa414fb-fd52-455b-b582-850dfa3c9bc9/.

Chappell, Bill. "Japanese Climber Junko Tabei, First Woman to Conquer Mount Everest, Dies at 77." NPR, October 22, 2016. https://www.npr.org/sections/thetwo-way/2016/10/22/498971169/japanese-climber-junko-tabei-first-woman-to-conquer-mount-everest-dies-at-77.

Frenette, Brad. "A Final Interview with Junko Tabei." *Outside*, October 20, 2017. https://www.outsideonline.com/2252936/junko-tabei-anniversary.

Horn, Robert. "No Mountain Too High For Her: Junko Tabei Defied Japanese Views of Women to Become an Expert Climber." *Sports Illustrated*, April 29, 1996. https://vault.si.com/vault/1996/04/29/no-mountain-too-high-for-her-junko-tabei-defied-japanese-views-of-women-to-become-an-expert-climber.

"Junko Tabei Special Feature," *Gakujin* (岳人) January 2022, 895.

Keiser, Ann B. and Ramsay, Cynthia Russ. *Sir Edmund Hillary & the People of Everest*. Kansas City, MO: Andrews McMeel Publishing, 2002.

Kurtenbach, Elaine. "Japanese Woman Scales Mountains While Ignoring Society's Stereotypes." *Los Angeles Times*, March 31, 1991. https://www.latimes.com/archives/la-xpm-1991-03-31-mn-2258-story.html.

Mt. Everest Conquered – Japanese Women's Party Bathed in Glory (エベレスト 女の栄光：豪華カラー日本女子登山隊写真集). Tokyo: The Yomiuri Shimbun (読売新聞社), 1975.

Otake, Tomoko. "Junko Tabei: The First Woman Atop the World." *Japan Times*, May 27, 2012. https://www.japantimes.co.jp/life/2012/05/27/people/junko-tabei-the-first-woman-atop-the-world/.

Tabei, Junko. *Honouring High Places: The Mountain Life of Junko Tabei*. Translated by Yumiko Hiraki and Rieko Holtved with Helen Y. Rolfe. Banff: Rocky Mountain Books, 2017.

Tabei, Junko. *I Like High Places* (高いところが好き). Tokyo: Shogakukan Bunko (小学館文庫), 2007.

Tabei, Junko. *Life Has Peaks and Sometimes Valleys* (人生、山あり時々谷あり). Tokyo: Ushio Publishing, (潮出版社) 2015.

Tabei, Junko. *Mountain Vocabulary Book* (山の単語帳). Tokyo: Sekai Bunkasha (世界文化社), 2012.

Tabei, Junko. *Ms. Tabei, We are on the Summit* (タベイさん、頂上だよ　田部井淳子の山登り半生紀). Tokyo: Yama-kei Publishers Co. (山と渓谷社), 2012.

Tabei, Junko. *To the Mountains, Refreshingly* (爽やかに山へ). Tokyo: Tokyo Newspaper Publishing (東京新聞出版局), 1997.

Tabei, Junko. *Yet I Still Climb the Mountains* (それでもわたしは山に登る). Tokyo: Bungei Shunju (文藝春秋), 2013.

Tabei, Masanobu. (田部井政伸) *Summit: The Life Philosophy of My Wife, Junko Tabei* (てっぺん　我が妻田部井淳子の生き方). Tokyo: Takarajimasha, Inc. (宝島社), 2017.

Tokyo American Club. "Peak Passion." *iNTOUCH*, February 2014 (Issuu, January 29, 2014). https://issuu.com/intouch_magazine/docs/intouch_feb2014.

Yoshikawa, Mai. "Mountain Queen Not Done Yet." *Japan Times*, February 25, 2003. https://www.japantimes.co.jp/news/2003/02/25/national/mountain-queen-not-done-yet/.

Yuikawa, Kei. (唯川恵) *Junko's Summit* (淳子のてっぺん). Tokyo: Gento-sha (幻冬舎), 2017.